T0156653

Perfectly Imperfect

Seven Pieces of Advice to a More Fulfilling Life

Michael A. Pickles

Order this book online at www.trafford.com
or email orders@trafford.com

Most Trafford titles are also available at major online book retailers.

Print information available on the last page.

isbn: 978-1-4907-9162-3 (sc)
isbn: 978-1-4907-9164-7 (hc)
isbn: 978-1-4907-9163-0 (e)

Library of Congress Control Number: 2018912358

Trafford rev. 10/15/2018

 www.trafford.com

North America & international
toll-free: 1 888 232 4444 (USA & Canada)
fax: 812 355 4082

Preface

I would like to share a personal story with you, a story I feel demonstrates the decisive message behind this book, *"Perfectly Imperfect:* **Seven Pieces of Advice to a More Fulfilling Life***"*. As you will clearly see, the events in this story engrained the seeds for this noteworthy book.

In the summer of 2000, I willingly departed the comforts of Nova Scotia, Canada in exchange for an eye-opening, life-changing opportunity to participate in an educational development project in Guyana, South America, on behalf of the Canadian Teacher's Federation. The assignment was called *"Project Overseas."*

The name Guyana is an Amerindian word meaning *"Land of Many Waters."* It is the only country in South America with English as its official language. Not surprisingly, it is famous for its Kaieteur Falls, measuring five times as high as Niagara Falls. I highly suggest you pay Guyana a visit ... it's a beautiful country.

Our six-week assignment was to help improve the teaching methods of Guyanese teachers. Specifically, we were responsible for helping them prepare for their upcoming teacher certification examination. Passing this exam meant a pay increase, and since so many lived in poverty, passing was a major priority.

As I sit here and reminisce about my incredible learning experiences in Guyana, I find it hard to believe it was so many years ago. I can still vividly recall the day I was eating lunch with the other Canadian teachers when a convoy of large, military looking trucks pulled into the schoolyard. We all stopped eating and rushed to witness what was happening.

Once parked, the drivers rushed to the back and pulled up the worn, dust-covered tarps. We could not believe our eyes. Hundreds of people exited from the backs of each of those trucks. "Who are these tired, sick looking people?" I asked. Our Supervisor pointed out that they were the Guyanese teachers. They were the teachers who had traveled hundreds, even thousands of miles to be our students.

I was amazed and impressed with the tireless dedication of these teachers towards life-long learning. Many of them made the long journey with their entire families, had not eaten in days, were cramped beyond endurance, and undergone the journey through physical illness. They truly understood and appreciated the value of an education. Now **that's** dedication.

Soon all the teachers were unpacked, showered, fed, settled into their quarters and ready to begin classes.

The first two weeks were full of lectures, notes, and assignments, which I had planned in the comfort of my own home. I really felt as though I was making a world of a difference in the lives of these less fortunate, less educated Guyanese teachers. Suddenly all that changed.

One rainy afternoon, I was slowly packing up my teaching supplies when I was distracted by the voice of a woman. As I turned around to identify the soft-spoken voice, I saw the face of an older woman. In fact, I was certain she was young, but she looked much older. Maybe it was due to life's burdens and hardships, I wondered. She politely approached me, her eyes staring at the floor as if she was ashamed. I stood there silently and waited as she walked towards me. Finally, she stopped in front of me and asked one simple question, a question which would forever change my core beliefs.

"Do you have one spare pencil so that I may break it in half and give it to two of my students?" Not five, not ten, but one pencil is all she asked. Those words brought tears to my eyes. Not having a pencil to offer, and not knowing exactly what to do, I absently searched inside my wallet and gave her a "**Hug Someone You Love Today**" card. She smiled, looked at the card, gently took it from my hand, hugged me lightly and slowly walked away.

As I watched her leave the classroom, I realized something very important. It struck me how materialistically rich we are in North America, but often spiritually poor. I realized that although we North Americans may have far more money to spend on our educational system, those so called less fortunate teachers had one very important resource to offer their children ... their love. This and other incidents of kindness and sincerity in Guyana left me convinced that these teachers truly love their students and they truly love to teach. I promised myself that I would take this experience back to my teaching, back to my students. I had to do something. In the words of Helen Keller, *"I am only one, but I am still one. I cannot do everything, but I can do something. I will not refuse to do the something I can do."*

There is no doubt in my mind that the Guyanese teachers did learn from us that summer, that we did increase their pedagogical knowledge and improve their teaching skills. Fortunately for me, I learned just as much, if not more from them. I left all my teaching materials there and I proudly returned to Canada with so much more to offer my students ... more love and hope.

I would like to conclude with a story of the Chinese bamboo tree, which I read in a book from my favorite author and speaker, Zig Ziglar. The Chinese plant bamboo; they seed, they water and fertilize it, but the first year nothing happens. The second year they water and fertilize it, and nothing happens. The third and fourth years they water and fertilize it, and still, nothing happens. The fifth year they water and fertilize it, and sometime during the fifth year, in a period of approximately six weeks, the Chinese bamboo tree grows roughly ninety feet.

"Did the tree grow ninety feet in six weeks or did it grow ninety feet in five years?" Of course, it grew ninety feet in five years with the constant nourishment and the unfaltering devotion of the farmer. Now imagine your students as the bamboo seed and you, the teacher, as their water and fertilizer. In your hands, you hold the seeds of failure or the potential for boundless growth. What a huge responsibility, but what a great privilege as well.

Personally, there is nothing else that I would rather be doing with my precious time than offering hope, self-improvement, motivation and re-energizing both myself and others in life. The purpose of this books is to inspire you to be happy, to live a life filled with purpose and to act. As you read this book, hopefully, you will begin to feel more peaceful and more loving yourself. Life doesn't just happen- you make it happen. So, go out there and challenge yourself. Make mistakes, travel, read, inspire others, and live life to the fullest. Just don't forget to be kind to yourself, your family and friends, and to the environment along the way.

Re-read *"Perfectly Imperfect:* **Seven Pieces of Advice to a More Fulfilling Life"** as many times as necessary to stay enriched, motivated and inspired. This book is my personal gift to you. Until our paths cross again, remember what Ralph Waldo Emerson once said, *"What lies behind you and what lies before you are tiny compared to what lies within you."*

The next time you feel like giving up, think about the Chinese bamboo tree or those dedicated, persistent Guyanese teachers ... and don't forget to carry a few EXTRA PENCILS!

Acknowledgments

To say this book was solely written by me, Mike Pickles, is far from accurate. No book can be written without the input of so many others. So many people have influenced some of the ideas that this book would surely not have been written without you. So, thank you to everyone for your generous contributions.

A genuine thank you goes out to my publishing team at Trafford Publishing, who offered guidance with the corrections, revisions, and deadlines. A special thank you to my check-in coordinator Drew Navarro, who kept me informed and on track. Thank you all so very much!

A special thank you goes out to Sebastian and Cooper, who help keep me young at heart, and to my life partner, Denise, who inspires me daily to become a better person than I was yesterday. I love you all dearly!

I may have forgotten to mention others who have helped me with the writing, editing and publishing of this book, so please accept my apologies and know that you are all greatly remembered and appreciated.

"The roots of all goodness lie in the soil of appreciation." ~Dalai Lama

Mike the Author

Michael A. Pickles was born in Digby, Nova Scotia, Canada. He has been teaching for 24 years from K-12, as well as an Administrator, and at the college level. He was fortunate enough to teach in all three of Canada's territories; the Yukon, the North West Territories and in Nunavut. He has also taught overseas in Malawi, Africa and in Guyana and Ecuador, South America.

Mike has been published in numerous newspaper articles, had several radio interviews, was published in Reader's Digest: Our Canada, and was co-authored in a book entitled "*The Path to Success*" alongside The Secret guru Sandy Forster. His first book "**Hug Someone You Love Today: And How to Leave Your Personal Signature**" was a great success, which led to the publication of his second book, "**Hug Someone You Love Today: And the Simple Certainties of Life.**" These two publications led to his third book, "**Perfectly Imperfect: Seven Pieces of Advice to a More Fulfilling Life.**"

Mike is currently the Chair of Academic Upgrading for Northern Lakes College in scenic Peace River, Alberta, Canada. Besides his loving family- reading, writing, speaking, self-development and travel continue to be his greatest passions in life.

Mike also operates a motivational, public speaking business called *"New Beginnings Consultant."* If you require an enthusiastic, alluring, high energy speaker for your next engagement, you may contact him directly at mike_sabbie@yahoo.ca.

Perfectly Imperfect

Seven Pieces of Advice to a More Fulfilling Life

Many authors will tell you that one of the toughest phases of writing a book is finding the precise title that clearly defines the essence of your book- its true meaning. At least that challenging undertaking was true for me. I thought long and hard about my book title, and being somewhat of a perfectionist, I changed the title numerous times and, I'm still not convinced it's the right one. Nevertheless, I finally decided upon **Perfectly Imperfect,** because as humans we are imperfect beings, but perfect in our own ways, and that's okay.

Some of us can keep our failures and imperfections to ourselves, keep them hidden- for a while. However, none of us are perfect- not one. Sometimes we deal with our problems, our imperfections by completely reframing them, but they're still there. Don't fool yourself. We don't succeed in life because we have no weaknesses, no imperfections. We succeed because we find our strengths within those imperfections and develop them. Ron Scolastico once said, "If you would go every day to a very large tree and take five swings at it with an ax, no matter how large the tree is, it will eventually fall." The same principle applies to our life imperfections. Work on them daily and they will diminish, they will improve. Sharpen your life axe.

As I write this book, I am eleven months away from turning 50 years old. The BIG 50! Half a century old– so you can just imagine how excited I am. Please allow me a moment to digest that thought. 50 years old- how the hell did that happen? Father Time sure snuck that in. (Insert a loud yell and a door slamming) Okay, I'm back, I can breathe again, and I feel much better. On a lighter note, it has been said that if you don't grow up by 50, you don't have to. I guess I'm off the hook.

As I cautiously contemplate upon the increasing bald spot on the back of my head, and the unavoidable ageing process, I took some time to reflect upon what insights did I make (sometimes agonizingly) that I may want to pass on? Specifically, what tidbits of life advice can I offer the world to help support them along their life passage? Everybody's life journey is different, so take whatever advice you feel is relevant to your specific needs and disregard the rest. I will not be offended, especially since I am not the type of guy you want to put on speaker phone. Yes, I can be opinionated. Seriously, we are all on our own life journeys. What's yours?

Consider that thought for a minute ... if you have children of your own (nieces, nephews or grandchildren), what life lessons would you want them to learn from you? This is a very momentous question, especially since our early programming affects our future. The more I reflect upon it, the more I know I would have valued receiving such treasures when I was a young teenager. I may have avoided some pointless, mindless slip-ups and life haunting experiences.

In the prudent words of actor and filmmaker Jack Nicholson, "I hate giving advice because people don't listen anyway." I hope you regard the following seven pieces of advice I offer to help you live a more fulfilling life. Advice I'd surely tell my thirteen-year-old self.

1. **You Are Enough**
2. **Life Is Your Responsibility**
3. **Take More Risks**
4. **Never Stop Learning**
5. **Travel More**
6. **Open Your Heart**
7. **Live a Life of Balance**

"One of the basic rules of the universe is that nothing is perfect. Perfection simply doesn't exist. Without imperfection, neither you nor I would exist." –Stephen Hawkings

LIFE TIP: MAKE SURE
EVERYBODY IN YOUR
"BOAT" IS ROWING AND
NOT DRILLING HOLES
WHEN YOU ARE NOT
LOOKING.

1. YOU ARE ENOUGH

Are you enough? Am I enough? According to the Webster's Dictionary, the definition of **enough** is, "Occurring in such quantity, quality, or scope as to fully meet demands, needs, or expectations." Or maybe you prefer the Michael Jackson hit song, *"Don't Stop Til You Get Enough."* I'll let you decide for yourself what defines enough.

I once read an article in a Science Journal stating that if you can't find something to be grateful for, think of the human body. Your heart pumps over 1.5 million gallons of blood each year through 50,000 miles of blood vessels to nourish all your vital organs. Compare that to Canada's Horseshoe Niagara Falls that sees 600,000 gallons of flowing water daily. The heart is truly amazing, and so are you.

Although I have never met and will probably never meet most of you reading this book, I would like to assure you that whatever you do, where ever you are, you are enough. There is nothing you must prove to convince others that you are enough. You do not have to prove it to anybody because you are already enough. In Psychological terms, *Atelophobia* is the fear of imperfection in oneself, of not being enough. Don't allow this fear to take over. You deserve better. Actually, stop reading, stand up and confidently yell out to yourself, "**I Am Enough.**" Maybe don't do this in public to avoid being arrested but try it. If you honestly don't feel that way about yourself, keep repeating it until you do. This simple adjustment in your mindset will drastically alter your life.

If you think you're too small to make a difference, try going to sleep with a mosquito trapped in your tent ... bzzzzzz. Exactly, now you see my point. All kidding aside, in this world you will encounter difficult tasks and challenging people who will want to test you. Accept these challenges and give them your absolute best, but whatever happens, do not allow your self-worth to decrease in any way. When things get tough, and they will, you can start to doubt yourself. You may wish you were stronger, faster, and smarter, that you could do more, and that you had better support. Don't worry, no matter how much you may not feel like it, you are enough, and you will get through this- regardless of what ever *this is*. As the saying goes, "Tough times don't last, but tough people do." Become that person.

As mentioned previously, you are worthy, and you are enough. When you know your true self, you realize this fact as truth. I highly encourage you to make this your daily affirmation or daily mantra- **I AM ENOUGH.**

Repeat it until it becomes a part of your inner being. Repeat it until you believe it.

Dr. Wayne Dyer, one of my favorite authors and speakers, said it best. He said that we should stop interfering in our own lives, that everything we need is within us already, and that the universe will provide anything else that may be missing. He further states that we had everything we needed within the first 9 months of our lives, while still in our mother's womb. We had all the nutrients we needed, our temperature was perfect, our heart beat flawlessly without any thought, and we developed as needed. A little miracle bundle. We had everything we needed- we were enough. Why isn't that true for the rest of our lives? Because we interfere, we allow others to interfere, and we stop believing.

I suggest you stop interfering and start believing in yourself- believe that you are enough, because you are. In the stirring words from David Goggin, an American ultramarathon runner, ultra-distance cyclist, triathlete and retired United States Navy SEAL, "We live in a society where mediocrity is rewarded." Don't think in terms of "woulda, coulda, shoulda." Don't think mediocre, think big because you are enough.

Some of our best motivational gifts come incased in sandpaper. Embrace your inner struggle by taking the first step, change your attitude, and become honest with yourself. The first person you must be transparent with is yourself. Stories of success and hope inspire people to find their way out of a bad situation. Stories of how it was then, how it is now, and the magic that happens in between offers hope- gives us direction. Become your own success story.

It is said that in flying, the attitude of the airplane is what pilots call the position of the aircraft in relation to the horizon. Attitude living, like attitude flying, says that attitude dictates performance. Often our attitude is the primary force that will determine whether we succeed or fail. A positive attitude will certainly help you develop your own success story.

Speaking of success stories, I'd like to share a story I read a few years ago. It's about a man named Roger Bannister. Until 1954, the common belief was that man could not run the mile in under 4 minutes. It could not happen; it was not possible because it had never been done before. Well in 1954, Roger Bannister broke that benchmark, and since that time, over 20 000 other runners have also broken that record. Why? What changed?

Those 20 000 runners who lined up at the starting line believed it was possible, and so they made it so. As for me, I think running is great because you forget all your problems, cause you're too busy focusing on one problem- breathing! Seriously, I want you to believe that you are enough and that your dreams and goals are possible. Don't wait for the ideal situation; there will never be an ideal situation. Do what you can NOW with what you know, and with what you currently have.

Once you get over that first obstacle, that first wall, you'll know it's possible. You'll then carry that success and mental toughness onwards to your next obstacle. You will become a stronger version of yourself. That energy will lift you, will draw like-minded people towards you and will propel you towards your goals and dreams. Nothing will stop you now- you are on the move!

For you boxing fans– in Mike Tyson's prime, no other boxer could last five rounds with him. Once Buster Douglas knocked him out, other boxers began knocking Tyson out as well because they realized if you could last five rounds, you could beat him. Same in life– you must build resilience to go those extra rounds. You want your life to be a marathon, not a 100-yard dash. In order to do so, find your Roger Bannister from within.

Repeat the following sentences from motivational speaker and author Lisa Nichols. She states proudly, "I'm perfect in my imperfections. This is my time and I am enough." Remember where there is struggle, there is growth, and there is life. Believe you are already enough for greatness. Don't be average, and don't be mediocre.

Always do your best and seek growth. Better yet, go above the rest, because YOU ARE ENOUGH!

> **"Cowards don't start,**
> **The weak don't finish.**
> **Winners don't quit."**
> **~The National Guard**

Mike's Personal Reflection

There were many times in my life that I felt I was not enough, not good enough. For instance; I completed my Bachelor of Arts degree- not enough. I completed my Bachelor of Education degree- not enough. I completed my Master's in Education degree- not enough. I proceeded to take numerous other courses, certificates, diplomas, etc. – still not enough. Why? Says who?

Yes, there is always pressure from friends, family, your employment and society to do more, but honestly most of the pressures came from within, came from me. I placed these barriers upon myself. Maybe it was due to fear, low self-esteem, the need to perform, comparing myself to others, I'm not sure. However, once I began feeling that I was enough, it set me free. I now take courses because I want to learn, I want to better myself, I want to grow, and not because I feel any sort of pressure from any external forces.

It is a simple shift in one's mindset, but a very influential variation. Simon & Garfunkel said it best in their timeless, 1964 song *"The Sound of Silence"*. They sang, "Hello darkness my old friend. I've come to talk with you again." If any of those thoughts enter your mind, kick them out, and remind yourself that you are enough and that you are not alone. Give yourself a push, a wakeup call. Sometimes we need it, and sometimes we need to give it.

Do you share a similar life experience or thoughts? As you read my personal reflection, did it stir up any memories of your own? If so, you are certainly not alone. Most of us, if not all of us, have feelings of not enough, especially with the relentless influence of social media. Remember that no matter how bad it is or how bad it gets, you are going to make it. You will be okay. Please grab a pen and paper and refer to the Personal Action Plan section. It says action because you must actually "do" something. Are you feeling it? Let's begin.

Personal Action Plan

What actions can you take today- immediately, to change your mindset towards the thought that you are enough? Examples may be to take a course, read a self-help book such as this one, talk to a counsellor, forgive a friend, visit a family member, or take an exciting trip, etc. The options are endless.

Do yourself a favor, put everything aside, (including your cellphone) find a quiet place, take a few minutes, and write out an "***I Am Enough Action Plan***". Whatever it is for you, do it today- as in right now and I promise it will positively transform your life forever. Are you ready? From the lyrics of the 1976 hit sitcom Laverne & Shirley, "On your mark, get set, and-go now"

YOU ARE ENOUGH
"You were born enough, nothing you say or do
will ever add or subtract from who
you are." -Jenny Layton

LIFE TIP: YOU MAY BE GIVEN A CACTUS IN LIFE, BUT YOU DO NOT HAVE TO SIT ON IT.

2. Life is Your Responsibility

Responsibility is one of those terms you have certainly heard so many times from your parents that it goes in one ear and out the other. It may even be a word you fear and ignore because it can be quite heavy. Nevertheless, without it as a base, it may be easy to wander. Not taking responsibility may be less demanding, and it is far easier to blame your life problems on someone else. However, there is always a price to pay when you do not take full responsibility for your own life- such as given away your personal power. Think about the last time you refused to take responsibility for your life, and how that experience ended.

You are 100% responsible for how your life turns out. Maybe not how it began, but how it turns out. What you create out of your life; your happiness, your relationships, your success, your health, your wealth, everything is in your hands.

I love what J.K. Rowling says, "There is an expiration date on blaming your parents for steering you in the wrong direction; the moment you are old enough to take the wheel, responsibility lies within you."

Life is full of peaks and valleys, and we learn through our failures, weakness, challenges and life lessons. Accept that fact, and don't seek comfort- seek life instead. You've got to take personal responsibility for YOUR life. Yes, you will fail, yes you will make mistakes and have setbacks, but that's no reason to quit. Don't concern yourself with FEAR, because it's only False Evidence Appears Real.

You can influence and create your life the way you want it to be. You are the author of your own life, you hold the pen to rewrite it if that's what you desire. Your thoughts are your creative power to design your life how you want it to be. Don't waste that privilege. Think things through and then do what you need to do. Have the courage and take responsibility for yourself.

This may be a validating relation to low self-esteem. Instead of taken responsibility for one's actions, someone else is blamed and a victim mentality is created and empowered. That's dangerous. This harms many vital agencies in your life, such as relationships, yourself, future employment, etc. Does this resonate with you? It has with me. We all know that this victim mentality will not stop until you take back responsibility for your life. There is no easy solution, you must put in the honest, hard work. However, the transformation is remarkable, and you will feel so much better about yourself, increasing your self-esteem along the way.

This is also a noble way to stop depending on external confirmation like praise from other people to feel good about yourself. Instead, you start building strength within which energizes your life with positive emotions no matter what other people say or do. Personally, I use a lot of positive quotes. I surround myself with encouraging quotes to lift me up whenever I'm feeling low and to remind myself to take responsibility of my life. It's easy to do, and it's so effective. As they cautiously say in AA, if you don't want to slip, don't go where it's slippery.

Often you are the opposition in your path to success. You begin to self-sabotage yourself. I'm certainly guilty of this. Are you? To help eradicate that inner resistance, you must think that you are deserving, you are truly worthy. You may promote this process by using affirmations or other positive techniques, but the biggest sway comes from taking responsibility for yourself and for your life.

By taking responsibility for our lives, we not only increase control of what happens, it becomes expected to feel like you deserve more in life. As your self-esteem grows, and as you do the right thing on a regular basis, you feel better about yourself. It's a positive cycle. This is favourably important.

It is often said that your thoughts become your actions. Without taking responsibility for your life, those thoughts often remain silent and are not rendered into action. Taking responsibility for your life is that extra component that makes taking action more natural. You do not get trapped in thinking, you become proactive instead of passive. I've played a lot of sports over the years and I have found that the one device that seems to separate winners from losers more than anything else is that winners take action, they take responsibility. As the saying goes, "If your ship doesn't come in, you swim out to it."

You cannot control every outcome of your actions, and you cannot control how someone responds to what you say or what you do. Identify where your limits are, otherwise you may create a lot of pointless anguish for yourself and others through wasted energy by taking responsibility for what you never really could control. Please be mindful of that difference.

Life comprises of the simple things each day, not just the big events. So, do not forget to take responsibility for the small things today and do not delay them. Admittedly, taking responsibility for your life can be hard and challenging on you. It is not something you master overnight, but I think you'll agree that it is so rewarding. It is also a lot of fun and the payoff is massive. Why? Because you are no longer trying to escape from your life. Instead, you face head on what is going on, triggering new life possibilities to open up for you. That's exciting!

Improvement is not about occasional short spurts; regular action is what really pays off and can help you achieve just about anything. For instance, working out in the gym. You may gain some benefits from intense, long workouts. I've fallen prey to that mentality myself. But you'll gain far greater benefits if you moderately work out consistently every day, building up that true 'farmer strength." In the long haul, consistency is always more beneficial than intensity. It wins out every time. Don't believe me, ask the turtle and the hare. The hare is still losing sleep over that race.

Furthermore, through consistency you build your self-esteem to developed levels, and may notice that many smaller complications you repeatedly experience such as negative thinking start to right themselves as your self-esteem improves. You gain inner strength creating positive feelings within yourself without validation from other people. That my friend is an extremely valuable asset.

How do you take responsibility? There are many ways, but it is a choice that you must make. Doing the correct thing in every situation is hard to do. It really is. I suggest you do not aim for perfection, instead be as good a person as you can be. When you have this line of thinking, it becomes easier to stick with taking responsibility and to not justify to yourself that you did not have to take responsibility. That does not mean that I beat myself up, I just note that I can do better. That way I become less vulnerable to echoing the same mistakes.

In my opinion, there are two ways to approach life-one is to wake up and say I want predictability, the other is to say I want new adventures in my life and I am responsible. Seriously ask yourself which one you prefer. The moment you take responsibility for your life is the moment you can change anything in your life. LIFE IS YOUR RESPONSIBILITY!

Mike's Personal Reflection

There is only one person responsible for the quality of the life you live- that person is YOU. You must decide what it is you want, believe you deserve it, and go for it. This is highly important, so let me say that again. Decide what you want, believe you deserve it, and go for it.

I shamefully admit that I did not take personal responsibility for my relationship with my own mother. Yes, my mother left us at a very young age, yes, she was an alcoholic, and yes, we were vastly separated geographically. However, looking back now, those were all overused excuses on my end. Excuses I used to circumvent the situation in front me- my collapsing relationship with my mother.

Many years later, and now that I have children of my own, I realize that denying myself that responsibility and hiding behind a wall of excuses backfired in a big way. How? My mother died before I had the chance to mend our broken relationship, before I had a chance to say you did the very best you could, before I had the chance to say it's okay, before I had the chance to say I love you. I did not man up and take on that responsibility, a decision I'll regret for the rest of my life. If there is a responsibility in your life that you are not owning, I say step up right now, face it, and deal with it. It will truly set you free.

It's been said that you will never go forward until people are behind you. More importantly, you will never get ahead until you are behind yourself. Like it or not, we all must make those tough, responsible life decisions. I will most likely regret my decision for the rest of my life, but that's on me, I own that. However, I do not want anyone to feel the colossal regret and guilt that I do in regards to my relationship with my mother. So please grab a pen and paper, and honestly complete the Personal Action Plan section.

Personal Action Plan

First understand one thing, you are not the first person (nor will you be the last) who has fallen short with their personal or life responsibilities. As you read earlier, I am also guilty. Cut yourself some slack, ask yourself some truthful questions, forgive yourself, and move forward. In life, mistakes and failures don't matter. What truly matters is moving forward and growing from our mistakes, our life experiences- good or bad.

What are you avoiding so that you do not have to take responsibility? What's holding you back? Stop blaming others, cut the excuses, take down your wall of defenses, and take responsibility for your life and make the changes you really want to see. We can only deal with what is in front of us today, so take responsibility today. Life can change in an instant, so please don't hesitate.

Compose a *"Responsibility Blueprint"*. Write a list of everything you have been avoiding, everyone you have been blaming, and personally check off that list until its blank. Each action step you take will bring you closer to the life you should be living, the life you deserve to be living. Do it now!

TAKE RESPONSIBILITY

"Man must cease attributing his problems to his environment and learn again to exercise his will— his personal responsibility." -**Albert Einstein**

LIFE TIP: SOMETIMES WE
MUST BURN OUR BRIDGES
SO THAT WE NEVER CROSS
THEM AGAIN.

3. Take More Risks:

Either we grow from the pain of loss or we grow from the joy of pleasure. It's been said that to become old and wise, one must first be young and foolish. Either way, there's growth. I ask you which experience would you prefer? In the words of Joseph Joubert, "When you go searching for honey, expect to be stung by bees." In other words, taken risks is not easy, and you may get hurt, frustrated, and discouraged, but don't let that stop you. Despite all those unknown factors, keep taken risks and keep failing forward. Your life will open up as a result.

Why would anyone want to leave this journey here on earth with gas still left in their tank? You will never reach your full potential until you get out of your comfort zone, so take risks. Play full out, don't hold back, and give your all so that when your time expires, you'll know that you gave it your absolute best. South America's first black President, Nelson Mandela, nailed it when he said, "There is no passion to be found in playing small, in settling for a life that is less than what you are capable of living." I say taste every fruit on every tree in the garden.

What gives you the most pleasure and makes you feel purposeful? What is it that when you finish doing it, you immediately feel fulfilled? What is it that you do that makes time stand still? Whatever that is, take the calculated risks necessary and do more of it. Maybe start part-time but do more of it. The clock is ticking my friends, our lives are on loan, and we're living on borrowed time that could expire at any moment. We may not have control over how we are going to die, but we certainly have control over how we are going to live.

Remember that our days are precious currency of your life. Spend them wisely. Don't think like Homer Simpson when he says, "Trying is the first step towards failure." Instead, think more like Steve Jobs as he so eloquently advised, "Your time is limited, so don't waste it. Don't be trapped by living with the results of other people's thinking." Look at the enormous success of Apple. Steve Jobs certainly did not allow fear and others to detain him, he lived outside the box.

Certainly, Ray Kroc, the founder of McDonald's, would not have been so successful if he didn't take risks. Although many did not believe in his fast food concept and the desire to eat out, Ray believed in himself and took the risk regardless.

He standardized operations, ensuring every hamburger would look and taste the same in Toronto as in Tokyo. He set strict rules on how the food was to be prepared, cooking methods and times, portion sizes and packaging. Ray Kroc took the risk and built the company into the most successful fast food in the world.

Today, McDonald's restaurants are found in 119 countries around the world and serve more than 64 million customers a day. What's even more amazing about his story is that Ray accomplished this idea at the ripe age of 52. "If you have time to lean, you have time to clean," Ray would often say.

If you're not impressed with hamburgers and cheeseburgers, look at the story of Sam Walton, a humble businessman from Arkansas. He began building his dream with a single dime store. Walton slowly built his business step by step until a quarter of a century later he had accumulated a chain of 38 Wal-Marts.

According to the Forbes Global 2000 list, Wal-Mart is the biggest private employer in the world with over 2 million employees and is the largest and most successful retail store chain in history. To be that successful, Sam clearly took risks. Now you don't have to become another Ray Kroc or another Sam Walton, but I do encourage you to take risks and to live your life to the fullest.

Years ago, I concluded that what we fear doing is usually what we need to do the most. Furthermore, we often succeed by the number of uncomfortable actions/risks we are willing to take. Think of a time when you

felt 100% alive, undistracted and in the zone- get there
again. Take the time to find something that calls to you.
No more excuses- take the necessary risks. Your life will
change profoundly once you do.

Have you ever watched the Claymation movie
"Chicken Run", starring chickens trying to escape
their destiny on the chopping block? At times this same
principle applies to us- these limiting fences are not real,
they are all in our minds. The following inspiring youth
have proven that to us. Please make it your undertaking
to check out these incredible youth founders and TAKE
MORE RISKS!

Craig Kielburger- Free the Children: fighting against
child labor and fighting for international human rights.

Hannah Taylor- The Ladybug Foundation: raising
money for food, shelter and the needs of the homeless
population

*Julian Goza, Desi Aardema, Jared Brechot, Nico
Cardenas, and Kelly Hanen – Teens Helping Kids:*
raising money to meet the needs of impoverished
children in their home community.

Alexandra Scott- Alex's Lemonade Stand: raising
money for cancer research.

Janine Licare and Aislin Livingstone– Kids Saving the Rainforest: raising money to save the rainforest and the endangered animals who live there.

Annie Wingnall– Care Bags Foundation: creating care packages for children removed from their homes by agencies and placed into another home.

Austin Gutwein– Hoops of Hope: organizing a basketball shoot-a-thon to raise money for orphaned children due to AIDS.

Olivia Joy Stinson– The PEN Pals Book Club: organizing a literacy-focused association intended to support the children of inmates.

Kyle and Garrett Weiss– FundaField: raising money to build soccer fields in Kenya, Uganda, and South Africa.

Jackson and Tristan Kelley– Backpacks: collecting backpacks with school supplies for kids in need.

Abigail Lupi– CareGirlz: singing and performing in assisted-living centers to cheer up the elderly.

Anthony Leanna– Heavenly Hats: collecting hats for cancer patients to wear that have lost their hair due to chemotherapy.

Mike's Personal Reflection

Several years ago, I was teaching elementary school and I recall a grade six student telling me she wanted to become the next Prime Minister of Canada. What an ambitious goal. Her parents lovingly encouraged her, as did I and her other teachers, which reinforced that you can become anything you put your mind to. I think we can all agree what a wonderful response.

However, if you're 50 years old (like I soon will be) and announce you're leaving your secure job to start your own business or to become a writer, the response is drastically different. You're told to be realistic, to get serious, get your head out of the clouds and remain at your current secure job. In my case, I was told I must be going through some sort of mid-life crisis. Ouch! I'd prefer the encouraging response that was giving to that grade six student.

Why is that? Why can a child dream big, shoot for the stars and be encouraged for those dreams? Why is an adult discouraged and shot down for those same dreams? There are many reasons why and that is not the focus of this dialogue. My argument is to encourage you not to stop dreaming, to think like a child, to dream big, and continue to take risks as you grow older.

As for myself, I was well into my early forties when I decided to write my two books, *"Hug Someone You Love Today,"* and began my motivational speaking business *"New Beginnings Consultant."* Why did I wait so long? Because I doubted myself, listened to the naysayers, and cowardly put my dreams aside.

No more, now I take risks as often as possible. I enjoy challenging myself, I enjoy newness, I enjoy pushing myself outside of my comfort zone, and I've personally grown so much as a result. I hope I was (still am) a worthy mentor to my children and they live a fulfilling life as a result. I also wish and desire the same for you, so roll that dice and take a risk!

Personal Action Plan

Like I have many times in my life, don't get caught up in the routines, in the life ruts- get out of your comfort zone. Once a year, I challenge you to take a risk, to do something different, something so challenging that it will greatly influence the next 364 days of the year. Not only will you be experiencing amazing, new life adventures, but will always have something to look forward to. If once a year becomes too easy for you, then do it several times a year. Only you know how much life altering changes you can handle.

Think about that. Truly reflect on that challenge. This exercise may be difficult, but I promise you if you do it, the rewards will be awe-inspiring. Recently I tried parasailing with friends and family. It was breath taken. I'm not a big fan of heights, so it was terrifying, but I took the risk, conquered my fear of heights and felt empowered as a result.

Sometimes, our lives must be completely shaken up, changed and rearranged to position us to the place we are truly meant to be. I challenge you to sail away from your safe harbor. What life changing risks will you take? Write it down, tape it to your mirror where you'll see it daily and make it a reality.

RISK TAKING

"Twenty years from now you will be more disappointed by the things you didn't do than by the ones you did." -Mark Twain

**LIFE TIP: IN LIFE,
DO WHAT MAKES
YOU REALLY HAPPY!**

4. Never Stop Learning

Every morning we get a chance to change, a chance to learn, a chance to be better than yesterday. If you are like me, you enjoy learning and willfully engaging in lifelong learning "just because." You are intrinsically motivated to learn and therefore do not need a list of potential benefits. I personally believe it is its own reward. As an educator of over 24 years, I have had many students come to me and say, "Mr. Pickles, how much is this assignment worth." To which I'd confidently respond, "No mark can compare to how much this is worth, it's a learning experience, which is worth a lifetime."

I justly feel you should continuously educate yourself. Education is one of the finest things you can do to make sure you head into the right direction in your life. Get a great education and learn what fascinates you. Find your passion in life and check if you can make a living from it. For me it is educating and empowering others through my books and seminars. What's your passion? Feeding one's mind means giving your mind input. I encourage you to be open to new stimuli, different perspectives, remain curious, study the past greats, and never stop learning something new.

It has been said that Walt Disney never took a formal course in his life. In 1923, at the age of twenty-one, he moved from Kansas to Los Angeles to work in the movie business, but no one would hire him. He had no experience. So, Walt rented a camera, set up a studio in his uncle's garage and taught himself to make animated cartoons.

By 1934, Walt created full-length animated feature films, such as Snow White. In 1950, he entered television with the Mickey Mouse Club, and in 1962, he launched a new theme park- the magical world of Disneyland. Through all of this, he was self-taught, he taught himself what he needed along the way. I acknowledge that not everyone can become a Walt Disney, but you can become your best.

Conversely, most people equate learning with a formal education at school, college, university, etc. We are told, at an early age, that we need a decent education. It is true that a formal education, and the accompanying credentials may maximize our potential to find better jobs, earn more, and become prosperous in our chosen career. However, formal schooling is only one form of learning. There are so many other opportunities to advance your knowledge and develop your life skills. For instance, home schooling, online courses, start your own business, travel, participate in real life experiences such as Habitat for Humanity, etc. Feel free to add to this list. What other types of learning have you been involved with?

With the popularity of the internet today, knowledge can be attained and skill-sets acquired anywhere and anytime. I'm amazed at what I've witnessed my 13-year-old son learn on YouTube. Even I have performed various do it yourself, handy man projects around the house due to YouTube videos. Projects that have saved me hundreds of dollars, maybe even thousands. What a colossal sense of freedom. However, lifelong learning is about forming and sustaining a positive attitude to learning both for professional and personal growth. Lifelong learners are motivated to learn because they want to, (such as myself). Lifelong learning can enhance our appreciation of the world, offer us better opportunities and expand our quality of life. That's no joke.

Learning is such a personal entity. Always think, "Is there a better way of doing this?" For instance, maybe you've taken the same route to work for many years. One day you venture to take a different route and realize not only is it much faster, but far more scenic. This slight change saved you gas, time and offered a more pleasant view. Use that same line of thinking in other areas of your life.

If you are a hockey fan, you'll appreciate this next reference. I recently read the book, *"Nine Lessons I Learned from My Father"*, a book about Mr. Hockey, the legendary Gordie Howe. Throughout the book, he brilliantly describes the nine characteristics of Mr. Hockey, which are; live honorably, live generously, play hard, have patience, live selflessly, be tough, stay positive, and be humble. Whether you are a hockey fan or not, those nine lessons can certainly apply to all of us, and especially to learning.

Promise me, better yet, promise yourself that whatever you learn, do so with gratitude and a positive attitude. Maybe you heard the story about three people working side by side on a construction site. All three were asked the very same question, "What is your job?"

The first person never looked up, and quickly said, "My job is to do what I am told for eight hours per day, so I can get myself a paycheck."

The second person replied, "My job is to crush rocks, and I am a great rock crusher."

The third person looked up with a gentle smile and said with outright pride, "My job is to build a stunning basilica."

Three people, all doing the same job, but with different attitudes. Which of the three men do you think would be the best long-term employee? Although the first person can perform many tasks and the second can crush rocks, the third person will likely be the most devoted.

The odds are he/she will have a greater sense of job satisfaction because they understand their purpose and how it fits into the bigger picture. Have you ever asked yourself how you fit into the bigger picture at your current job?

Note that nobody achieves anything great by giving their minimum, without making sacrifices, and without giving their best. Always try again, try harder and fail forward. You won't believe what you can achieve by attempting the impossible. The more you know, the more you grow, and the more you sow. Never stop learning.

As part of my life-long learning, I try to find mentors. Although I have never met any of them, (I hope to one day) in their own way, they have each taught me so much about myself and about life. It is my hope that you take the time to read about some of them. It will be a treasured use of your valuable time, and NEVER STOP LEARNING.

Zig Ziglar – although a successful background in direct sales, he is the world's foremost authority on motivation. His I CAN Course and books such as *"See you at the Top"* and *"Better than Good"* have made him an internationally renowned speaker. I really like his comment, "You can have anything in life you want if you'll just help enough people get what they want."

Dale Carnegie – one of the most well-known authors in the field of public speaking and communication, and best known for his book "*How to Win Friends and Influence People*", as well as the Dale Carnegie Institute. Words of wisdom from Dale, "You'll never achieve real success unless you like what you're doing."

Maya Angelou – a memoirist, poet, and civil rights activist. She published seven autobiographies, several books of poetry, three books of essays, and was credited with a list of movies, plays, and television shows. What a powerful quote from Maya when she articulates, "I've learned that people will forget what you said, people will forget what you did, but people will never forget how you made them feel."

Napoleon Hill – many credit Hill's book "*Think and Grow Rich*" as the foundation for their personal and financial success, and millions today continue to learn from his audio programs and books. Words of advice from Hill, "Plans are inert and useless without sufficient power to translate them into action."

Norman Vincent Peale – became an innovator in the self-improvement industry by connecting the power of positive thinking with action. This led to his bestselling book "*The Power of Positive Thinking*." Norman would often say, "Even people who have a long record of not succeeding can be turned into tremendous achievers if they will discard their images of themselves as failures."

J.K. Rowling – a British novelist, film producer and screenwriter and best known as the author of the Harry Potter fantasy series, which have gained worldwide attention, selling more than 400 million copies, becoming the best-selling book series in history. In her words, "We do not need magic to transform our world. We carry all of the power we need inside ourselves already."

Earl Nightingale – spent much of his life searching how a person, starting from scratch, with no advantage, can reach his lifetime goals. In doing so, he produced a spoken word record called "*The Strangest Secret*". Earl alleged, "We can let circumstances rule us, or we can take charge and rule our lives from within."

Jack Canfield – one of America's experts on peak performance and developing self- esteem, and of course most known for the "*Chicken Soup for the Soul*" series which he co-authored with Mark Victor Hansen. Jack states, "Get started now. With each step you take you grow stronger, more skilled, more self-confident, and more successful- but you have to take action to get it."

Mark Victor Hansen – has been called one of the top 10 greatest motivational speakers, and widely known as the Chicken Soup guy due to his publishing phenomenon of *"The Chicken Soup"* book series. In the words of Mr. Hansen, "You can easily create the life you deserve."

Louise Lynn Hay - a motivational author and the founder of Hay House. She has authored several New Thought self-help books, including "You Can Heal Your Life."

She is a powerhouse in daily affirmations, such as the following, *"Love is the great miracle cure. Loving ourselves works miracles in our lives."*

Deepak Chopra – one of the top 100 icons and heroes of the century and is nationally recognized in the holistic health field for popularizing *Ayurveda* or natural healing. In the words of Deepak, "Let's bridge the technological miracles of the west with the wisdom of the east."

Stephen R. Covey – widely acknowledged as one of the world's leading authorities on empowerment, and best known as the author of *"The 7 Habits of Highly Effective People"*. Stephen keeps it simple in expressing, "The main thing is to keep the main thing the main thing."

Dr. Wayne Dyer – a philosopher and one of the most popular self-empowerment speakers and authors in the world, and best known for his best-selling book *"The Erroneous Zone"*. Wayne believed deeply that, "You're the creator of your thought, which means that in some metaphysical way, you're the creator of your life."

Spencer Johnson – has helped millions of readers discover how they can enjoy better lives by using simple solutions. Also, the co-author of the best-selling books" *"Who Moved My Cheese?"* and" The *One Minute Manager"*. Johnson often said, "Look at what happened in the past, learn something valuable from it, and use what you learned to improve the present."

Anthony Robbins – considered the leader in human development training, Anthony Robbins is the best-selling author of many books and popular audio learning programs. His dynamic presentation style and messages appeal to millions. For instance, "People are not lazy, they simply have impotent goals – that is, goals that do not inspire them."

Jim Rohn – one of the most influential thinkers of our time and referred to by many as the greatest motivational speaker of all time. Rohn uses a "can-do" spirit. Consider the following; "Give to yourself the gift of patience, the virtue of reason, the value of knowledge, and the influence of faith in your own ability to dream about and achieve worthy rewards."

Barbara Walters – a television personality, broadcast journalist, and author. Walters has hosted the following television shows: Today, 20/20, The View, and she has co-hosted the ABC Evening News. She always tries to see the good in people. *"To feel valued, even if only once in a while, that you can do a job well is an absolutely marvelous feeling."*

Les Brown – a motivational speaker, radio DJ, author, former television host and former politician. Although declared "educable mentally retarded" while in grade school, he learned how to reach his full potential - a key point in his many motivational speeches. As a motivational speaker, he uses the catch phrase "It's Possible!" and teaches people to follow their dreams.

Brian Tracy – his seminars on leadership, goal setting, motivation and time management have earned him as one of the leading authorities on personal effectiveness, and the development of human potential. His views concerning achievement can be echoed in his statement, "There have never been more opportunities for you to turn your dreams into reality than there are right now."

Mike's Personal Reflection

Although I highly value my Bachelor of Arts degree, my Bachelor of Education degree and my Master of Education degree, some of my most memorable learning experiences were via informal education. Free online courses such as how to become a better speaker, or how to write/publish a book have become invaluable to me. Attending seminars on leadership and communication have also served me well. Reading books on self-help and human development were tremendously helpful. Watching documentaries on YouTube or listening to podcasts while I drive to/from work have opened my mind. If you want to learn, the opportunities are infinite.

I used to read a lot, but unfortunately have cut down over the years. Today I do more selective reading. Basically, choosing books with innovative ideas and messages that are life changing. Below are my top 12 book choices that I hope you find the time to read. I promise they will be worth the effort.

1. *The Miracle Morning* by Hal Elrod
2. *The Monk Who Sold His Ferrari* by Robin Sharma
3. *Tuesdays With Morrie* by Mitch Albom
4. *The Power of Now* by Eckhart Toole

5. *The Power of Positive Thinking* by Dr. Norman Vincent Peale
6. *Think and Grow Rich* by Napoleon Hill
7. *Jonathan Livingston Seagull* by Richard Bach
8. *The 4-Hour Workweek* by Tim Ferriss
9. *Man's Search for Meaning* by Viktor Frankl
10. *How to Win Friends and Influence People* by Dale Carnegie
11. *Awaken the Giant Within* by Tony Robbins
12. *Hug Someone You Love Today* by Mike Pickles ... I had to sneak that in

As I grow older, I realize that lifelong learning is a necessity for me- I truly thirst for new learning opportunities. Although I have been an educator for 24 years, I most likely will never seek out another degree or diploma via formal education, such as in a college or university setting. I am not saying that it is not important, because it is for so many. However, I prefer informal methods such as those I mentioned earlier. They simply resonate with me far better. You may be different and that's okay. Select the method that works best for you.

Personal Action Plan

Make your new learning motto, "**Discover and Uncover.**" I challenge you to learn something new at least once a month, preferably twice a month. You don't have to attend college or university, it could be as simple as taken a class or a course in your community.

Start off by thinking small and build from there. Some examples are: taken a course at your local library, a free online course, guitar lessons, cooking lessons, dance lessons with your partner, learning a new language, scuba diving, etc. What have you always wanted to learn? Don't worry about failure, focus on the learning opportunity.

Over the years, I've learned so much from my mistakes, that I'm thinking of making many more. Remember that the body has limitations, but the mind does not. The skies the limit.

LIFE-LONG LEARNING
**"Beautiful thing about learning, nobody
can take it away from you." -B.B. King**

LIFE TIP: REALIZE THAT A YEAR CAN COMPLETELY CHANGE A LOT FOR A PERSON.

5. Travel More

When was the last time you traveled? Where did you go? Did you enjoy it? What did you learn? Are you planning a trip within the next year? If not, I highly advocate that you do. In my view, travel is one of the greatest freedoms we have. I don't mean going home to visit the parents and raiding their fridge for groceries but truly traveled. Real travel is when you take to the open road and accept what ever comes your way. It's a form of condensed education helping us make sense of the world.

There are undeniable, scientifically proven health benefits to traveling. Intellectually, emotionally, and physically, you will improve massively simply from packing your luggage and visiting places you've never seen before. It works for me. I absolutely love traveling. I can't get enough of it. It's my addiction. If you know of a job that will pay me to travel, sign me up. If you haven't traveled lately, here are a few reasons why you should that may sway your decision.

Traveling is a confidence builder. It really is. The first few trips may seem overwhelming and awkward, but the more you travel, the easier it becomes. For instance, as you overcome the difficulties of learning a new language, exchanging local currency, or figuring out foreign cultural customs, you are building confidence. You are also becoming more independent and increasing your ability to acclimatize to a range of circumstances. Those life skills, such as confidence, may be transferred into your everyday life. I cannot stress this enough- traveling is an ultimate confidence builder.

In 2004, I sold my house and most of my belongings to live and teach in Quito, Ecuador. For two years I lived in a predominantly Spanish speaking environment, a country where I had no family, or personal connections. Although daunting at times, especially due to the culture shock, what an amazing, eye opening, and life-changing experience it was. I highly recommend it to everyone. Not necessarily Ecuador, although a great choice, but moving to any foreign country. It truly changed me forever and I'm certain it will do the same for you. What country would you select?

When I returned home, I moved to northern Canada, Nunavut to be exact. The idea of that move may have overwhelmed me before living overseas, but then I said to myself, "If I can make it abroad in a foreign country, I will be okay in a northern dwelling where I at least share the English language, same currency, values, etc. Through traveling abroad, I felt that I can do this, regardless of the challenges, and suddenly those hurdles seemed less obtrusive and far more welcoming. Through travel, I not only increased my confidence, but I developed a humbling sense of the world- that is a worthy cause. Wouldn't you agree? I believe that becoming more culturally sensitive is crucial in our globalizing world. A good example is when I was teaching in Malawi, Africa for one summer. My coworkers, whom I had invited for supper, would arrive 1-2 hours late. Some people may view this cultural norm as being lazy, (I did at first) when it really has a lot more to do with the fact that Malawians value connection over time. Stopping to connect with family and friends along the way was far more important to them than rushing to be on time.

I feel that us North American time worshipper could truly benefit from their cultural value of human connection. We tend to value time too much, sometimes at the detriment of human connection. What time is it now? Did you look at your watch? Being aware of cultural values and norms can greatly help us apprehend international issues. It is an important ability to be able to shift and see where someone else is coming from. Cultural sensitivity will help you with that communication, which is made possible through travel.

Like it or not, with social media and the internet, we are quickly becoming globalized. It is not unlikely that you would end up with a job that has you travel for work or take part in a conference call with multicultural partners. I've participated in many myself. Therefore, it is helpful to be culturally aware and it can't hurt to know a foreign language. Having lived or at least traveled abroad can give you a competitive edge in the workplace.

Before I lived abroad, I never really appreciated the beauty of becoming proficient in another language. In Canada, most of us speak two languages, English and French. Once you travel overseas, especially in Europe, many individuals you meet speak multiple languages. Something I envy intensely.

Living abroad is the best way to learn a new language, since you are forced to practice your new skill daily. Not only does it open up employment possibilities, but a whole new world of people you can connect with either as friends, coworkers or even romantically. (Check out the endless online dating sites if you don't believe me) Traveling forces us to become more social. We all know that we desire more human connection in this fast paced, technology driven world. Travel can help create global friendships and make this big world feel much smaller, and more intimate.

In my mind, travel is a far better investment than any material things. The world is your playground. Mix it up- travel by car, plane, boat, bus, train or horseback. Follow the advice from the 1979 theme song of the Littlest Hobo.

"There's a voice that keeps on calling me
Down the road is where I'll always be
Every stop I make, I'll make a new friend
Can't stay for long, just turn around and I'm gone again.
Maybe tomorrow, I'll want to settle down,
Until tomorrow, I'll just keep moving on."

My message is simple. Become a true traveler of life. Be spontaneous, explore the world, hear other's stories, make memories, and TRAVEL MORE

Mike's Personal Reflection

I once heard the following quote at a Teacher's Convention, *"The best fishing is where the fewer people go."* If you fish, and I don't, that makes a lot of sense. Depending on your take in life, that simple statement could mean many things to countless people. For the sake of this topic, I'd like to apply it to traveling.

I have been fortunate enough to travel to every province and territory within Canada, to most states in the US, and to a few countries overseas. My bucket list is to visit many more foreign countries. I am aware that I have not traveled as much as a lot of people, but my goal is to continue gathering as many stamps as possible on my passport. I'm excited just thinking about it. Instead of Diego the Explorer, one day it will be Mike the Explorer. Maybe even turn it into my own reality TV show. Any TV Executives reading my book?

Although it's a lot of fun to travel to popular places such as the Eiffel Tower, Niagara Falls, the Great Wall of China, etc., I personally prefer the paths less taken. I prefer to ask a local, "Where's the best river to canoe, the best hills to hike, the best mom/pop eatery, or the best waterhole in town? I'm not saying that the Eiffel Towers of the world are not important, because they are, I simply prefer the unpopular or less visited areas. I personally learn more, feel more comfortable, and more connected in these environments. I'll leave it to you to pick your travel destination preferences, but please don't forget the least visited areas of the world.

The best advice I can offer is to meet as many people on your travels as possible. It will surely make your time abroad more enjoyable since the locals know best. Not only is it usually cheaper, you never know when these connections will come in handy in the future. I have made many wonderful friendships from traveling, many which we remain great friends to this day. Maybe one day I'll have the honor of meeting some of you- my readers.

Personal Action Plan

The Earth moves 1.6 million miles per day. I challenge you to be a part of that movement and start logging your miles. My challenge to you is to goggle places you'd like to travel. Speak to your family and friends about their favorite travel destinations, talk to a travel agent, grab a copy of The Lonely Planet from your local library, or simply spin the globe and blindly point to a country- wherever it lands, that's where you are going next. (I've done that before)

Give yourself six months, a year, or two years to save up for a travel fund and make it happen. Better yet find cheap or free ways to travel the world, such as listing your home with Airbnb, crew a yacht, or volunteer for an organization. Catch the travel bug, increase your Aeroplan points, and enjoy more of life. You will be thankful you did.

TRAVEL MORE
"All travel has its advantages. If the passenger visits better countries, he may learn to improve his own. And if fortune carries him to worse, he may learn to enjoy it." -Samuel Johnson

LIFE TIP: YOU CANNOT
CHANGE THE PEOPLE
AROUND YOU, BUT YOU
CAN CHANGE THE PEOPLE
YOU CHOOSE TO BE
AROUND.

6. Open Your Heart:

None of us are immune to emotional pain and heartbreak. The years 2013-2016 were very taxing, wearisome years for me. The fist two years were filled with energy, enthusiasm, excitement and a huge learning curve as I embarked upon a new job, forming new friendships in a new town. That all drastically changed.

On my terms, I resigned from my position, letting go of all my securities, but more importantly, letting go of a toxic job environment, and began a new life full of unknowns. I also began a journey of removing the splinters from my life. If something or someone was not making me happy and stronger, I removed them. Period. They say the hardest walk you can make is alone, but it's the one that will make you stronger. Truth be told, I was scared, but I was happy that I removed the toxicity and stresses from my life. Are you currently in a similar position?

A little voice inside my head, (No I'm not crazy) told me I had to do this, told me to forgive and to open my heart again. It wasn't easy. I had to honestly explore the barriers I put between myself and others. Sometimes it was sarcastic remarks, isolating myself, or becoming the joker in the room. I personally have used such behaviours to shut down and to hide my true inner feelings. Have you? I went into a protective, survival mode. Take a moment right now and identify your layers, your barriers, and your defensive behaviours to protect your heart. What are they?

Time is the only thing we cannot get back. Life is short, so please don't put yours on hold. Through opening my heart, I was finally connecting with my true self, my true soul, finding my bliss, and following my inner passion- becoming a professional speaker and author. I honestly never felt better and more alive! Who are you waiting to forgive?

People sometimes come into our world for fleeting moments and leave us forever changed. For better or for worse, we have more power to create or to destroy than we can imagine. We can leave things or individuals better or worse than we found them. I have had my heart broken many times and I have hurt other's hearts as well, but I chose to forgive, to open my heart and move forward with love and hope. Opening our heart is scary, nerve racking, terrifying and leaves us vulnerable, but it is so worth it. In every bad experience, there's always a valuable lesson to be found. Until you change your state of mind, you'll repeat the same mistakes from your past. And unless you change your present, your past will predict your future.

What justifies spending the best years of your life hoping for happiness in the last? Do not save it for the end, there is no reason. Suggestion for all you writers out there. As soon as you think it, ink it. In other words, keep a heart journal. Everything you experience today is a direct result of the choices you have made in the past. Pain is never far away if you are looking for it. Hang onto the positive ones and let go of the negatives. Write down your daily thoughts and feelings, especially those negative feelings that are holding you back. Write them down, then let them go- forever. It's not easy, I know, but it's possible.

The Greek philosopher Socrates sagely said, "Let him that would move the world first move himself." In other words, if you want to make an impact start with yourself and often the things that upset us in others are the lessons we must learn ourselves and OPEN YOUR HEART.

Mike's Personal Reflection:

"Life is too short to wake up in the morning with regrets. So, love the people who treat you right, forgive the ones who don't and believe that everything happens for a reason. If you get the chance, take it. If it changes your life, let it. Nobody said it would be easy, they just promised it would be worth it." – Dr. Seuss

What a great quote. It really sums it all up. Like many of you reading this book, we all have valid reasons why we should build a wall around our heart, let no one in, and to never get hurt again. I suggest you discontinue to search in the same rabbit hole of pain and refuse to be held hostage to your heartbreak. Trust me, I have felt that pain and fear for many, many years- far too long, and it didn't help or make me any happier. It served just the opposite.

Instead of reliving the 1978 song by Bonnie Tyler, **"It's a Heartache"**, I decided to find the courage to open my heart. Courage doesn't mean you don't get afraid. Courage means you don't allow fear to stop you. What's stopping you from opening your heart?

Personal Action Plan:

I challenge you to begin a Heart Journal. Write down an exhaustive list of all the names of people who have hurt you, and who you have hurt. Once you have that list, use it. Write them a letter, call them, or visit them in person if possible and tell them how they made you feel. Tell them that you forgive them, you hope they forgive you, and that you are positively moving on with your life without any bitterness.

Avoid any unnecessary searches for explanations. You are simply letting go. Be forewarned that they may never offer forgiveness, and that's on them, but you can do your part and forgive them. You are identifying your painful voids and filling them with positives. This will offer healing and closure- which is so powerful.

They say that to forgive is to set a prisoner free and that prisoner is YOU. If we truly want to love (and we all do), we must learn to forgive. Remember that forgiveness may not change the past, but it may change your future. Try it, you have nothing to lose, but so much to gain.

OPEN YOUR HEART
"Have a heart that never hardens, a touch that never hurts." –Charles Dickens

LIFE TIP: IT'S OKAY TO
LOOK BACK AND THINK
OF FOND MEMORIES, BUT
NEVER STOP MOVING
FORWARD.

7. Live a Life of Balance

I'm guessing you have either said or heard the following phrase many times, "There's just not enough time in a day to do everything I need to do." In today's high speed and high-stress world, a balanced work and family life is hard to find. It should not be, but it unfortunately is. Although I'm much better at it today, I still must consciously remind myself to keep a life of balance.

If you're a "stay-at-home" parent, you likely constantly struggle to find balance between the needs of your family and your own needs– for exercise, be alone, visit friends, even to take a long hot bath. On the other hand, maybe you are a single parent who is working so hard that you have trouble developing a social life, or even finding some down time for yourself. Or maybe you are so involved in partying that you fail to take care of your physical needs or the demands of your family. Only you know what category you fall into.

In Japan, a phenomenon exists called **Karooshi**, where people literally work themselves to death. Balance is a concern, and sometimes can become a matter of life and death. Stress can and will kill you. Please don't wait until you're at the tipping point, take care of your needs now. Find your balance.

There are so many things that we must balance in our lives; work, family, leisure, caring for others, caring for ourselves, social events, environmental issues, to name a few. "Finding balance" in our lives is so important, yet so hard, that there are mountains of books about it. A quick Google search of "How to find balance in your life" brings up 565,000,000 results. It's not hard to understand why we are searching for balance. The question is why are we having so much trouble?

There are a lot of answers to that question, including cultural ones that lead to uncertainties about the world we live in and anxieties about taking care of ourselves and our loved ones. If interested, there are hundreds of books available. I highly suggest you take the time to read a few of them.

There is one crucial point that many of these books seem to miss. Finding balance is a lifetime mission. It is ongoing and not a fixed goal. Balance is a way of living-it is a process with peaks and valleys. It helps to become aware of your relationship with time. The average lifespan in Canada is about 80 years old. If you're 50 (as I soon will be) you have another 30 years left to live. That's scary to think about, but it certainly puts things into perspective. I suggest you focus on what you really want to do with your last remaining 30, 40 or 50 years. Build your life resume, empty those heavy buckets that don't matter and live in the moment. Easier said than done I know. So, what can you do to find some balance in your life? That is a fair question, and I am no expert, but here are a few suggestions that may help.

As mentioned earlier, balance is an ongoing process. Being balanced does not mean being calm and relaxed all the time. Balance often occurs only for a passing moment. Rather than trying to stay balanced, think of yourself as practicing balancing. It is good to fall, to fail– it means you are trying. The same is true in life. As long as we keep practicing finding balance, we are moving forward. Examples may include exercise, yoga, meditation, prayer, or just a walk in nature. How you find balance is a personal choice. What's your preference?

Prioritize your life. Decide which items are most important, and then do the most important things first. Sounds easy doesn't it? The problem is figuring out what is most important. On any given day what is your priority? Is checking your work emails more important than playing soccer with your children? You decide, but to stay focused, you may have to re-examine your priorities. Say no to regrets for your time and stay true to what really matters- the bigger picture.

Be explicit. It is more beneficial to say, "I'm going to eat more fruits and vegetables throughout the day, and I'm going to exercise for 30 minutes Monday to

Thursday", than to say, "I'm going to eat healthily and exercise more." Be precise. The more precise you are, the easier it is to hit your goals, to find balance.

It is often easier to find balance with the aid of another person. Find a coach, or a partner for collaborative support. If you are carrying all the weight, it's likely you will not find balance. What is most important is not how much weight one-person carries at any given time, but how you interact with one another, giving energy to each other. It's been said that many hands make lighter loads.

Note that both accomplishments and disappointments are a part of balance, but we may not always give equal energy to each. If you are someone who typically focuses on your failures, try to notice instants of success. It is okay to fall back into thoughts that are more familiar, just go back to the positive ones when you can.

Balance is a never-ending challenge. It is different for everybody because you have different needs, so listen to your inner voice. Once you find the right balance for you, then life begins to flow effortlessly. It's like untangling a traffic jam. Live a life that you don't need to take a vacation from- find your flow.

To help put this into perspective, read the following story called, "Fables and Fortune Hunters," which I read in the amazing book, *"The 4-Hour Workweek"* by Tim

Ferriss. If you haven't read it, make sure you do. Its life changing.

An American businessman took a vacation to a small coastal Mexican village on doctor's orders. Unable to sleep after an urgent phone call from the office the first morning, he walked out to the pier to clear his head. A small boat with just one fisherman had docked, and inside the boat were several large tuna. The American complimented the Mexican on the quality of his fish.

"How long did it take you to catch them?" the American asked. "Only a little while," the Mexican replied in surprisingly good English.

"Why don't you stay out longer and catch more fish?" the American then asked.

"I have enough to support my family and give a few to friends," the Mexican said as he unloaded them into a basket.

"But what do you do with the rest of your time?" the American inquired.

The Mexican looked up and smiled, "I sleep late, fish a little, play with my children, take a siesta with my wife, and stroll into the village, where I sip wine and play guitar with my amigos. I have a full and busy life, senor."

The American laughed and stood tall. "Sir, I'm a Harvard M.B.A. and can help you. You should spend more time fishing, and with the proceeds, buy a bigger boat. In no time, you could buy several boats with the increased haul. Eventually, you would have a fleet of fishing boats."

He continued, "Instead of selling your catch to a middleman, you would sell directly to the consumers, eventually opening your own cannery. You would control the product, processing, and distribution. You would need to leave this small coastal fishing village, of course, and move to Mexico City, then Los Angeles, and eventually New York City, where you could run your expanding enterprise with proper management."

The Mexican asked, "But senor, how long will all this take?"

To which the American replied, "15-20 years, 25 years tops."

"But what then, senor?"

The American laughed and said, "That's the best part. When the time is right, you would sell your company stock to the public and become very rich. You would make millions."

"Million, senor? Then what?"

"Then you would sleep late, fish a little, play with your kids, take a siesta with your wife, and stroll to the village where you could sip wine and play your guitar with your amigos."

I hope this story serves as a wake-up call, and to reveal to you just how valuable your time is and how waiting for the future is never the solution. The harsh reality is that there are seven days a week and "someday" is not one of them. "One day you will wake up and there won't be any more time to do the things you've always wanted. Do it now." – Paul Coelho

Mike's Personal Reflection

As I referenced earlier, 2013-16 were difficult years for me. It was as if the life was being sucked out of me.

There were factors that negatively influenced interactions with my family. I could not sleep, was not eating, was losing weight, becoming angry and resentful- overall, my life balance had negatively shifted for the worse. Unlike the Mexican fisherman, my life was completely out of balance. I was like an iceberg flipping over on its end. I was drowning.

After that life changing experience, I now purposefully keep an eye on my work-life balance, and on my overall life balance. They say you have nothing once you lose your health, and in my case, that was true. I don't want that to happen to any of you, and if it already has- change it.

Personal Action Plan

Are you finding it increasingly difficult to keep your head above water? Is your life out of control? Are you stressed more than not? If you are finding it more challenging than ever to juggle the demands of your job and the rest of your life, you are not alone.

Even if you do not have much control over the hours you have to work, ask yourself, "What is important in my life?" Do a *"Life Balance Action Plan"*. Write a list of ways you can bring greater joy into your life and focus your attention on the things you can control.

By letting go of the things you cannot control, you will get closer to a life of balance- a life without unnecessary stresses. Take the wisdom of Jana Kingsford to heart, "Balance is not something you find, it is something you create."

A BALANCED LIFE
"Never get so busy making a living you forget to make a life." –Dolly Parton

LIFE TIP: ALWAYS REMAIN STRONG, BECAUSE YOUR STORY IS NOT OVER YET.

An Extra Nugget: Bonus Advice

Don't take life so seriously and I'm guilty of this myself. Don't worry so much about the bills, your hair, your neighbour's new car, and other's opinions of you. Live your life according to YOUR terms, not according to theirs. You only have one shot at this life, make your life matter- leave your legacy. To help you achieve this goal, answer the list of *"What If's."* Once complete, add your own ideas to the list.

What if money wasn't an issue? …

What if I found the woman/man of my dreams? …

What if I had the perfect career? …

What if I exercised more? …

What if? … You fill in the blank

I saw the following quote at a local drugstore. The words really struck me, so I wanted to share with you. "Life will always be complicated. Learn to live happily in the now, otherwise you'll run out of time."

Finally, in the words of my favorite comedian of all time, Robin Williams. *"You're only given a little spark of madness in life, you mustn't lose it."* God bless you Robin Williams.

Me as a young hockey player. I was never the fastest player or the top scoring player, but "what if" I never laced up a pair of skates?

Putting It All Together

In conclusion, everything that we encounter in life has something to teach us. Regardless of the circumstances of your current reality, you are the writer, director and producer of your life story. You do not have to struggle, you do not have to fight- just be.

In the words of the greatest boxer of all time Muhammad Ali, "I've made my share of mistakes along the way, but if I have changed even one life for the better, I haven't lived in vain." I believe each of us is born with a life purpose. My life purpose is to educate, inspire and empower people through educational seminars and by spreading the message of hope through my books. I sincerely hope to uplift humanity and leave the world a better place for my children and grandchildren. Sure, at times this undertaking is difficult and fearful, but I plug forward anyway.

When you are afraid to move forward, afraid to make that tough life decision, reflect upon the words of Robert Frost's advice in *The Road Less Traveled*.

> *"Two roads diverged in a wood, and I-*
> *I took the one less travelled by,*
> *And that has made all the difference."*

Before you close this book, please seriously reflect upon your golden carrot- what is your **so that** ...? For instance, I want to accomplish this, so that ... (Fill in the blank with your passion, your life's purpose) *What is your so that ...?*

I genuinely hope you enjoyed reading my book as much as I enjoyed writing it. This book is intended to be a call to action for you. I hope it was. Say goodbye to the past, to the old you. It's time to be happy, time for life changes- amazing things await you. I say life changing because I truly believe that if you honestly reflect and act- your life WILL CHANGE.

The best of luck with your life journey,
Mike Pickles

LIFE TIP: YOU CAN'T GO BACK AND CHANGE THE BEGINNING, BUT YOU CAN CHANGE THE ENDING.

Read YOUR Story in Mike's Next Book

In 1963, Edward Lorenz presented a theory to the New York Academy of Science. He stated, "A butterfly could flap its wings and set air molecules in motion, which move more molecules, ultimately capable of starting a hurricane on the other side of the world." That's a powerful effect.

Today we know this as The Butterfly Effect, and the same principle applies to people. I urge you to use the influence of your butterfly effect. I am putting together my next book called *"Success Stories"* and I would like all my readers to participate by sharing their own inspiring, life changing success stories.

Do you have a motivational story that you would like to share? Do you know of a friend or a family member who may have an inspiring story that you feel they should share? If you answered yes to the questions above, please send me your story. Stories from both young and old, male and female are equally welcome. There is no limit on how long your story must be, but please focus on quality versus quantity, along with a short permission letter to use your story.

Please send your stories to:

SUCCESS STORIES

mike_sabbie@yahoo.ca

"Don't let the fear of striking out hold you back." ~*Babe Ruth*

Other Books by Mike Pickles

You may purchase either of my Hug Books online via amazon.ca or indigo.ca or contact me directly at mike_sabbie@yahoo.ca for your signed, personalized copy.

"Hug Someone You Love Today"

Reader's Personal Notes

Printed in the United States
By Bookmasters